The Nature

of Leadership

Stephen R. Covey • A. Roger Merrill
Photography by Dewitt Jones

FranklinCovey

Franklin Covey Co.
2200 West Parkway Blvd.
Salt Lake City, UT 84119
(801) 975-1776
www.franklincovey.com

Manufactured in the United States of America by Publishers Press
Designed by Stephen Hales Creative, Inc.

ISBN 1-883219-90-6

Also from Franklin Covey Co.:

The 7 Habits of Highly Effective People
Principle-Centered Leadership
First Things First
Daily Reflections for Highly Effective People
First Things First Every Day
The Breakthrough Factor
To Do...Doing... Done
The Power Principle
The 10 Natural Laws of Successful Time and Life Management
The 7 Habits of Highly Effective Teens
The 7 Habits of Highly Effective Families
Franklin Planner

Acknowledgments

We gratefully acknowledge the contributions of many whose talents and dedicated efforts have made this book possible. We would especially like to thank:

- Rebecca Merrill, whose talent and judgment helped create every element of this book, and who especially helped refine thoughts and feelings and translate them into words. Except by choice, she could in every way be listed as a co-author of this work.

- Toni Harris, who has been committed and involved in many ways throughout the project. Her warmth and sensitivity in interviewing our contributors led to a deep, meaningful sharing and to rich friendships that go well beyond the last page of this book.

- Annie Oswald, for her coordination, counsel, and diligence, particularly during the last weeks of the book's creation and production.

- Blaine Lee, our close friend and associate, who first articulated and put into practice the elements of what has come to be known as the "Sundance Promise."

- Stephen Hales and his associates for their extra-mile effort and creativity in design and production.

- Interwest Graphics for their special care and concern in doing the drum scans of the transparencies.

- Publishers Press for their excellence in bringing the final product to fruition.

- Others whose encouragement, support, and help have played a vital role, including Stephen M.R. Covey, Greg Link, Janeen Bullock, Christie Brzezinski, John Azzaro, Boyd Craig, and Lynette Sheppard.

- Finally, our wonderful families. Only those who have been through a creative experience such as this know the price they pay to help make it happen.

In addition, we each could list many who have significantly affected us in our personal lives—people who have inspired us over the years with their insight, wisdom, and expertise, and who have instilled in us the desire to contribute to the lives of others. Truly, we stand—with gratitude—on the shoulders of giants.

Stephen R. Covey   A. Roger Merrill   Dewitt Jones

Come forth into the light of things,

Let Nature be your teacher.

WILLIAM WORDSWORTH

The Sundance Promise

If you will open yourself

to the natural environment,

the people around you,

and timeless principles,

you will find personal

and specific answers

to the leadership challenges

and opportunities you face.

Leader—or victim?

That's essentially the choice we all face today. And more than ever before, there's not much middle ground. Either we lead effectively—in our businesses, our families, our communities, even our personal lives—or we're tossed about by the circumstances and forces that surround us.

The challenges of today's leaders are significant. Global economy, high speed technological change, family instability, and increasing social problems create a host of new and complex challenges.

But there are fundamental principles or natural laws that create the basis of effective leadership on every level—personal, family, business, and community. And the ability to understand and apply these basic principles makes all the difference.

The Nature of Leadership is a book about the principles of effective leadership. But it's a different kind of book. It's not designed to be simply read; it's designed to be *experienced.* The message is powerful, practical, and immediately applicable. But, in addition to narrative, the message is communicated through photographs, experiences, and quotes.

The reason is simple.

In working with leaders worldwide, we've discovered that one of the best teachers of principles or natural laws, by far, is nature itself.

Nature is man's teacher.

She unfolds her treasures to his search,

unseals his eye, illumes his mind,

and purifies his heart;

an influence breathes from all the sights and sounds

of her existence.

Alfred Billings Street

So for many years, we have held leadership seminars in a variety of natural settings—most frequently at Sundance, Robert Redford's beautiful resort in the Rocky Mountains of Utah. To those who attend, we make what we've come to call the "Sundance Promise:"

If you will open yourself
to the natural environment,
the people around you,
and timeless principles,
you will find personal
and specific answers
to the leadership challenges
and opportunities you face.

We can make this promise with confidence because we've seen it fulfilled time and time again.

John Noel

President and CEO, The Noel Group

When I went to leadership training at Sundance several years ago, I was really struggling with some important issues in my life. As part of the outdoor experience, we went outside for a while, sat down under a tree, and just listened. It was very quiet. I could hear the birds. I could hear the snow falling from the trees. I could hear the wind blowing. And after a while, the thought occurred to me, "If I can be listening to the sounds of nature, why can't I be listening to other people?"

I realized that people were the most important part of my life, but I wasn't listening to them. As I thought about it, I came to the conclusion that I needed to do more listening and less talking. I needed to leave behind my feelings of defensiveness, feelings that I always had to be right. I realized that I could learn through listening, and that this would give me the freedom to do many other things in my business, such as putting together Win-Win Agreements and creating synergy with managers, executives, and customers. I became convinced that this was the one thing I needed to work on more than anything else—in my business, and in my personal life as well.

And so I did. I really worked on it, and I discovered that when you open your mind to listening to other people and really allow what they say to influence your thinking, it's very powerful.

The biggest difference I noticed was in my family. My wife and I had been headed in different directions. Our children were grown. I was focusing on business, and she was focusing on me... but I wasn't responding. I called her up and asked her to fly out to be with me. We sat under that same tree and talked and listened to each other. We shared each other's sorrows and joys in that natural setting, and it literally turned our marriage around a hundred and eighty degrees.

After we got back, I talked with my 22-year-old daughter on the phone. She was concerned about earning money for college and was going to get a job for six dollars an hour. Normally, I would have said, "Six dollars an hour? Great! Do it." And I would have hung up. But instead, I really tried to listen. I asked questions that went beyond the temporary six dollar an hour job and the next semester of school. We talked for an hour, and little by little, she really began to open up about her goals in life, her questions, and her concerns. Suddenly, she said, "Dad, you have never listened to me like this! I feel so good talking to you. You are really listening and it's really helping me. Thanks!"

Learning to listen has been a great help in business as well. As head of the organization, you find that over the years you end up being the old sage, and when people come in with problems, you immediately come back with a solution. But that isn't what people want to hear. They want you to really listen to them and to get to the point where they know you understand what they're talking about.

That's something I didn't do. I was always ready to tell autobiographical stories, to give immediate feedback. But now I really listen. I'm not thinking about what I'm going to say in the next statement or bringing in my own personal life. I'm letting people talk, and I can see in their eyes a sense of relief because they have finally found someone who will really listen and understand.

Also, I am much more open to third alternative solutions. In the past, I would come up with a solution and just do it. I didn't listen to other people. But now I practice listening to others and hearing their ideas. And many times it's not the first or second solution that's the best. It's not my idea or someone else's idea. It's a third alternative that's even better, and it comes through listening.

In my top left desk drawer, I have a little pine cone from that tree where I first got the message that I needed to listen. I look at it once in a while, and it helps me remember that even when I am under pressure, trying to get a lot of things done and moving quickly, I still need to take time to listen.

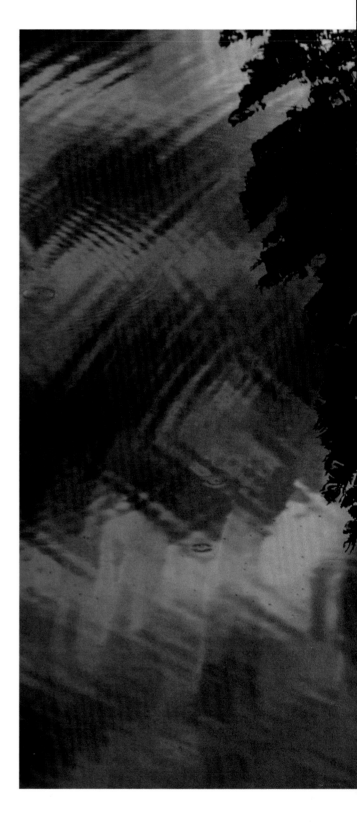

This book is our effort to bring the Sundance Promise to you. We've used beautiful nature photographs to invite you to see and experience the natural world. We've asked respected leaders from different arenas to share their

experiences to give you insight into the lives and discoveries of others. We've presented some of the basic natural laws that govern in all of life. And we feel confident promising that if you will open yourself to these three things, the Sundance Promise will apply to you. You will find specifically what you need to be a better leader.

Your path will be personal and unique. Everyone's is. That's what creates synergy and joy in relationships and sharing. As authors, we have traveled different paths.

For me (Stephen), nature has been a source of deep personal renewal, a place for nurturing family relationships, and a powerful metaphor for teaching the natural laws that govern in all of life.

For me (Roger), nature has been a prime regenerating power. It's also been the primary focus of one of my most enjoyable hobbies—photography—and a source of family bonding, as I've worked with my children over the years in the gardens and orchards of our mini-farm.

The two of us have learned from each others' perspectives, and our synergy has created new insights to apply in our shared focus on leadership.

We've also been thrilled with the additional synergy created in our collaboration with Dewitt Jones, an award-winning photojournalist who has spent much of his career on assignment for *National Geographic*. His love of nature and his search for ways to help leaders grow in creativity make him uniquely qualified to address this leadership focus. His insights and his beautiful images in this book (along with Roger's) help us all to "see" and connect with nature in a much deeper and more meaningful way.

Dewitt Jones

From the time I first picked up a camera, I have celebrated nature through my lens. And nature has responded by teaching me some extraordinary lessons.

Dewitt Jones

Early in my career, I came across the words of John Muir, father of our national parks and founder of the Sierra Club:

I used to envy the father of our race, dwelling as he did among the newmade plants and fields of Eden. But I do so no more, for I have discovered that I also live in "creation's dawn." The morning stars still sing together, and the world not yet half made, becomes more beautiful every day.

Much as I loved nature, my vision of wilderness was nowhere near that ecstatic. I thought, "John, you are either the master of hyperbole or something is going on out there that I need to find out about." So I went into the Sierra Nevada and lived there for 18 months. During that time I made a movie on John Muir's vision.

The first thing I discovered was that it was my eyes that were clouded, and that nature and life really were

just as beautiful as Muir had described, if I was open enough to see.

The second thing I discovered was Muir! Here was a man who walked into nature, saw its beauty and let it fill him up. He overflowed and it came out in everything he did— in the way he hiked the mountains, in his political activism, in his writing, in his huge agra-business in Martinez. It came out in his life.

Muir was a man who made his life his art, and that was a staggering concept for me. Like many, I had been raised in a school system that taught me from the time I was about knee high that there were two things: There was life…and there was art. And they were not the same.

Art was the ultimate elective. Art was what you got to do after everything else was done. Art was creative, and art was fun.

Then there was life. Life was serious. Life was hard. You were supposed to do life all the time. And those doing art? Well, they were a little suspect anyway.

What a terrible definition! I believe it defined most of us out of ever thinking that we could be creative. Creativity had to do with art, and art had to do with painting and sculpture, and if you didn't do those things you were out of the loop.

Muir showed me this wasn't true, that my creativity could come out in everything—in great photographs, in good business decisions, in the way I treated my family, in the service I gave in my community. It could come out in my life.

So nature taught Muir and Muir taught me, and "making my life my art" became one of the cornerstones of my creative vision.

And after all, *seeing* is the challenge. The lessons are all around us. They are also within us, for we, too, are a part of nature. Although most of us find it wonderfully refreshing to "get out in nature" and regret the time when we have to go back to the "real" world, the truth is that the world of nature *is* the "real" world. There are fundamental natural laws or principles clearly manifest in nature, and wherever we are, we live with the consequences of those laws whether we recognize it or not.

Throughout the history of the world and in many civilizations today, going "out into nature" would not be understood. You don't "go" to nature because you're already there. But in the past few centuries—primarily in the United States and Europe—the social/intellectual/emotional paradigm has been created that nature is somehow apart from us. Given the vast overview of human experience, the very fact that we even think of nature in this way is surprising.

It was not like taking the veil,

no solemn abjuration of the world,

I only went out for a walk and finally

concluded to stay till sundown

for going out I found that I was really

going in.

John Muir

The reality is that nature is where we're most at home. That's where life's most basic realities are clear. It's only when we try to feel at home in an artificial world, thinking we're in control, looking at life through a mechanical paradigm, trying to "fix" other people and find fulfillment in checking off "to do's" that we end up cynical and embittered, running faster and faster like a rat on a wheel.

As the saying goes, "fish discover water last."

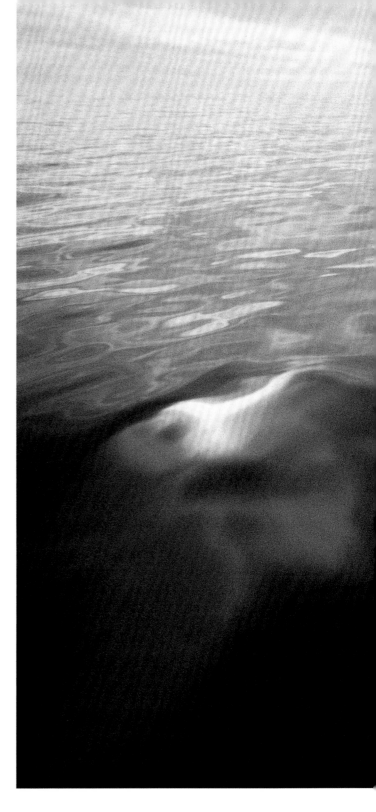

JoAnn Valenti

Author, professor, journalist

I've learned to time things so that I am driving with a beautiful sunset off to the west as I drive home. It calms me. It gives me a perspective. I think, "There is a hideous traffic jam in front of me. There are trucks on either side of me. This is a mess and I can't believe any good will ever come of it. But look at that phenomenal sunset! Look at those clouds. Look at the reflection on the mountains. Look at how it makes the snow sparkle on the mountains." It puts things in context.

Now we want to assure you that you don't need to go to Sundance—or any place in particular—to claim the Sundance Promise. In fact, many of the people whose stories we share have never been to one of our leadership programs. But they have learned to learn from nature.

When one tugs at a single thing in nature, he finds it attached to the rest of the world.

John Muir

Dr. Robert Schuller

Pastor, speaker, author

I believe that every living thing, whether it's a plant, an animal, or an insect, has its own natural habitat. And if it wants to be healthy and normal, it has to live within that environment.

A human being's natural habitat is a garden. It is in the garden that we are biologically realistic. When the eye sees the branches of a tree move slightly in the wind or the clouds move silently through the sea of space, or when the ear hears the sounds of rushing water or birds singing, it helps to tranquilize the soul. Tranquillity leads to dynamic, creative thinking and creative communication.

But human beings now are made to live with the sounds of engines, sirens, and whistles. Their eyes are forced to look upon a concrete world, car exhaust, power poles, telephone lines, clutter, and junk—all of which produce tension instead of tranquillity.

That is why I became highly involved in "biorealism" in American architecture. It's design for survival rather than design for opulence. It's where structure and space and people and environment have emotional interaction that is harmonious.

We have built the Crystal Cathedral in a 40-acre garden setting with waterfalls and pools. When you look through the ceiling, you see sunshine and blue skies. You do not see power poles or telephone lines. You cannot hear the sounds that generate tension. And I have had many spiritual experiences there.

I believe that almost all of my creative ideas have come when I was in tune with nature—in other words, emotionally and psychologically, I was in a garden. I have people say to me, "Yeah, but I live in the city. Where can I go to get these experiences?" You don't have to climb Mount Everest; you don't have to be at Big Sur. You can find tranquillity in a quiet place when the moon is full and it shines on your face.

It is an ecological, theological, and biological reality: The more we are in tune with eternal nature, the more we will be able to hear the still small voice within and have explosions of inspirational insight.

Douglas Spotted Eagle

International recording artist and lecturer

When we go to a studio and begin work on a record, those of us who are working closely often get together for some spiritual preparation. Since I live in the upper desert, we like to be outside.

With this last record, as we were going through this process, the air suddenly grew really still and quiet. It was almost as if we were in a vacuum and, except for the words of the holy man, there was dead silence. Then I began to hear sounds I never really noticed before. I heard some

birds begin to sing. I heard the rhythm of a train going down the tracks three miles away. The mountains lent a special echo to the sound of the wheels as they went by. I picked up one of the flutes and started playing with the birds and with the cadence of the train wheels going over the tracks. After about an hour—long after the train was gone, long after the birds were quiet—I had developed a whole new song.

Typically, when we go into working on a record, we write 20 to 30 songs and then select the best ones of the group. We had pretty well determined what we wanted to

I'm sure it's no different in the corporate world. You're constantly running at 100 miles an hour, giving 200 percent to whatever it is you want to achieve, and you're so busy running through the field that you forget to look at the flowers—the very thing that you are in. You forget to look at the thing you are creating from or inspired by. And pretty soon it becomes an exercise in mechanics instead of an exercise in creativity, wonderment, and beauty.

We have a set format now, where we will record for a certain period of time and then take a fixed break and go outside for a walk.

As I walk in nature, I talk to the things that are around me. I talk to the wind. I talk to the water. And I listen to what they have to say. In ancient times, long before you or I were born, we didn't have books. Our teachers, our professors, our lecturers, were the wind and the trees and the water and the animals. They all have something to teach us.

do on this particular album, but because of this experience, we ended up with a whole new song. It combined all of the important or sacred elements of Native American music with Anglo music, and it turned out to be the first symphonic piece in the history of Native American music that utilizes strings and traditional Native American vocals, flute, drum, and dance. This song, which has been performed by the Metropolitan Opera orchestra, has now become something of an anthem throughout the culture. And it would never have come if we hadn't stopped and listened.

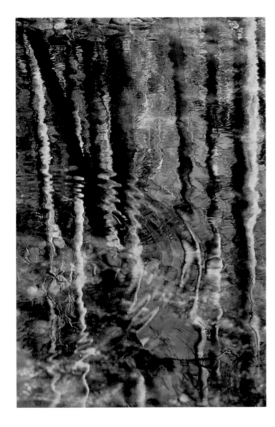

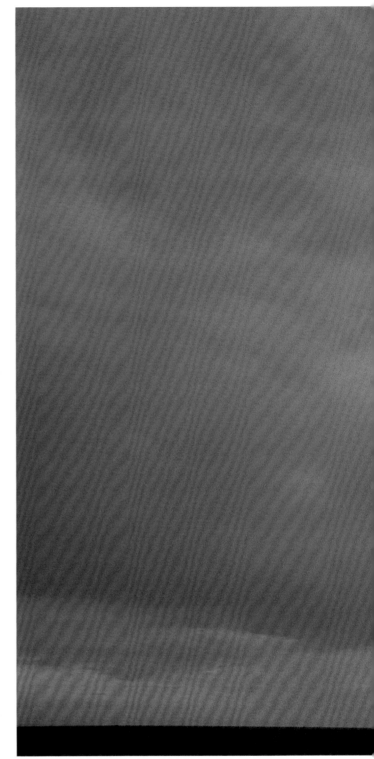

Beauty is before me.

Beauty is behind me.

Beauty is below me.

Beauty is above me.

I walk in beauty.

Navajo Prayer

The key is to be open, to really see what it is we're a part of.

Back in the third century A.D., the King Ts'ao sent his son, Prince T'ai, to the temple to study under the great master Pan Ku. Because Prince T'ai was to succeed his father as king, Pan Ku was to teach the boy the basics of being a good ruler. When the prince arrived at the temple, the master sent him alone to the Ming-Li Forest. After one year, the prince was to return to the temple to describe the sound of the forest.

When Prince T'ai returned, Pan Ku asked the boy to describe all that he could hear. "Master," replied the prince, "I could hear the cuckoos sing, the leaves rustle, the hummingbirds hum, the crickets chirp, the grass blow, the bees buzz, and the wind whisper and holler." When the prince had finished, the master told him to go back to the forest to listen to what more he could hear. The prince was puzzled by the master's request. Had he not discerned every sound already?

For days and nights on end, the young prince sat alone in the forest listening. But he heard no sounds other than those he had already heard. Then one morning, as the prince sat silently beneath the trees, he started to discern faint sounds unlike those he had ever heard before. The more acutely he listened, the clearer the sounds became. A feeling of enlightenment enveloped the boy. "These must be the sounds the master wished me to discern," he reflected.

When Prince T'ai returned to the temple, the master asked him what more he had heard. "Master," responded the prince reverently, "when I listened most closely, I could hear the unheard—the sound of flowers opening, the sound of the sun warming the earth, and the sound of the grass drinking the morning dew." The master nodded approvingly. "To hear the unheard," remarked Pan Ku, "is a necessary discipline to be a good ruler. For only when a ruler has learned to listen closely to the people's hearts, hearing their feelings uncommunicated, pains unexpressed, and complaints not spoken of, can he hope to inspire confidence in his people, understand when something is wrong, and meet the true needs of his citizens. The demise of states comes when leaders listen only to superficial words and do not penetrate deeply into the souls of the people to hear their true opinions, feelings, and desires."

Harvard Business Review, July/August 1992

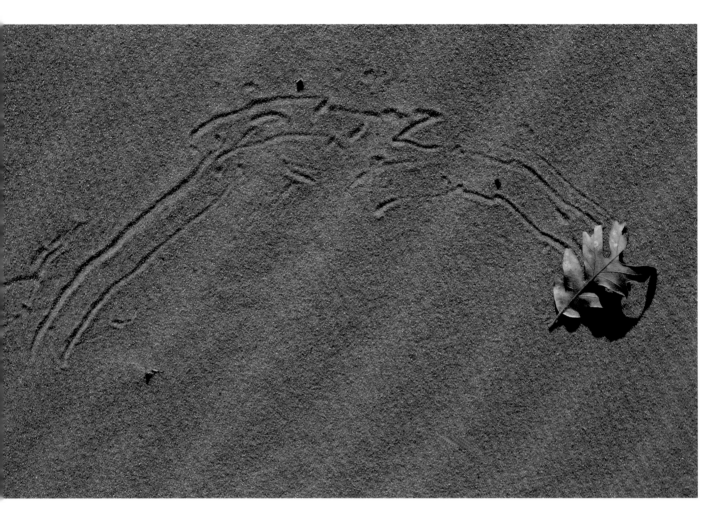

In the distant days when I was a boy scout, I had a troop leader who was an ardent woodsman and naturalist. He would take us on hikes not saying a word, and then challenge us to describe what we had observed: trees, plants, birds, wildlife, everything. Invariably we hadn't seen a quarter as much as he had, nor half enough to satisfy him. "Creation is all around you," he would cry, waving his arms in vast inclusive circles. "But you're keeping it out. Don't be a buttoned-up person! Stop wearing your raincoat in the shower!"

Arthur Gordon

A Touch of Wonder

As we become truly open, we discover that the essence of leadership is dealing effectively with the three constants in our lives:

Change

Changelessness

Choice

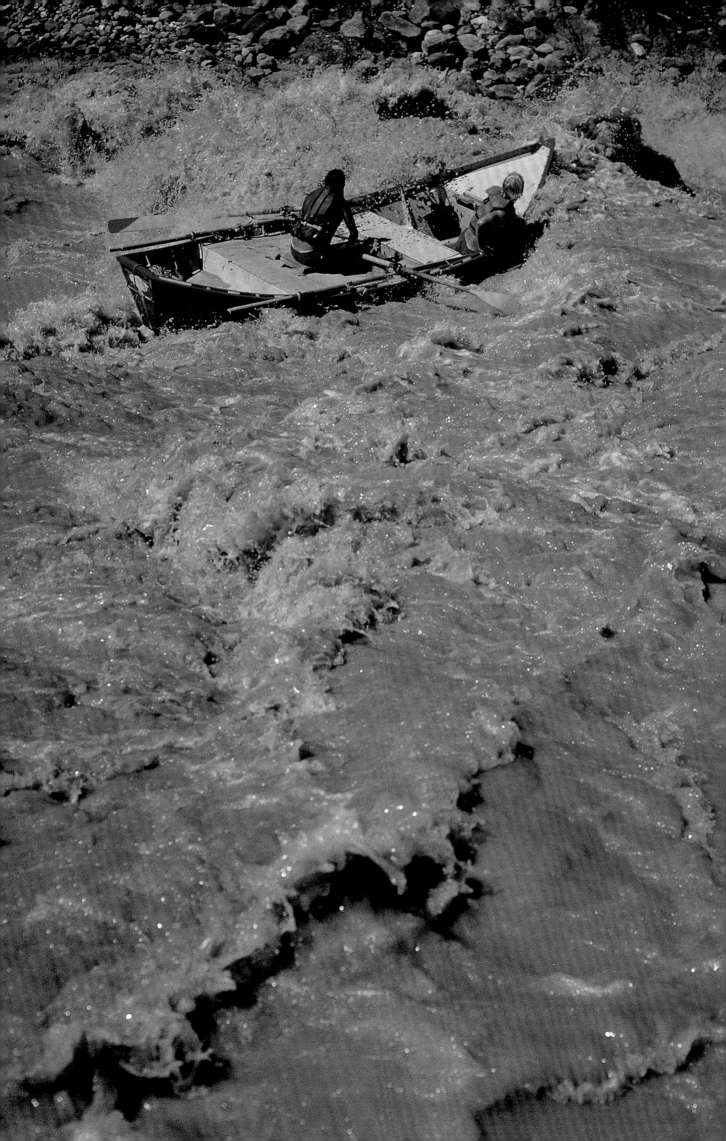

Change

Change is constant, complex, and often rapid. We can't control it. When we try, it becomes frightening, threatening. But we can learn to understand it, to work in harmony with it, to influence it, even to cultivate it.

Dewitt Jones

I dangled my hand over the side of the boat and touched it to the calm cold water. Instantly a small wake trailed off to the downstream side of my fingers, clear evidence of the river's unseen current. For six days, we had been running the Colorado River through the Grand Canyon in wooden dories. Besides the crew, there were 18 photographers on the trip, all participants in a seminar I was leading.

Perhaps it had been unfair to tell the participants I would be leading the trip. After floating for nearly a week, they knew that neither I nor the crew was really in control. It was the river that was in charge. It was its flow that we followed.

As we camped at Nankoweap, I asked the group to think about what it meant to "go with the flow."

"Going with the flow has taken on a whole new meaning for me down here," one woman said. "It doesn't mean turning off your brain; in fact, it's quite the opposite. It means being totally conscious, paying complete attention. For the boatman to survive a rapid, he must first realize that he's riding on a river over which he has little,

if any, control. If he believes he's the one directing things, he's doomed."

"Going with the flow also means knowing your own boat," offered another participant, "knowing everything it will and won't do, knowing its flip lines and first aid kit, making it an extension of yourself. If you don't know your boat, you'll never make it down the river."

"When I think of going with the flow," a third participant mused, "I am not on the river, I am the river—in touch with the source, straining at my borders, full of energy and serenity, ever changing, yet always the same."

For ten days the river teaches us its lessons…or maybe the river just is and we take what we need. In either case, when we finally return to the canyon's rim, what we have learned seems to glow not only from each transparency we have taken but from each of us as well.

Nature teaches that change is a vital part of life. Seeds change. Seasons change. Weather changes. People change. We are part of a dynamic, growing, ever-changing environment. Through change, we create better organizations, more productive teams, more harmonious families, better selves.

The problem comes when we try to create change as though we live in a static environment. We try to *fix* people, *install* programs, or *repair* relationships, as though they were isolated broken parts in some mechanical whole.

But the whole—the business, the community, the family, or even the individual—is a complex, highly interrelated ecological system. Each part has a living attachment to every other part. Change in any part affects all parts. When we learn to see leadership problems in terms of living systems, it dramatically changes the way we deal with them.

For the effective leader, change is a friend, a companion, a powerful tool, the basis of growth. Creating positive change is what leadership is all about.

Arun Gandhi

Grandson of Mahatma Gandhi,

Founder and President of the M. K. Gandhi

Institute for Nonviolence

From my early childhood in South Africa, I worked on the first farm community my grandfather started. At the time, it didn't make much sense to me, and it was hard for me to get up so early in the morning and work. But that experience taught me many valuable lessons.

I remember my parents and grandparents telling me, "When you plant the seeds and nurture them, they grow into healthy plants and give you fruit. They multiply. Soon you have a larger patch of whatever you want to grow." They said that in the same way seeds multiply when they interact with the elements of nature, our feelings and philosophies also multiply. To make the lesson more understandable, my grandfather would tell me this story:

An ancient king, curious to know about peace and non-violence, asked all the wise people in his kingdom to give him advice on the topic. All tried to explain as best they could, but none could satisfy his curiosity.

Eventually, he was told that there was a wise man who lived at the edge of town, but he would not come to the king. The king would have to go to him if he wanted an answer. So he went.

After listening to the king's question, the wise man went to the back of his house and came back with a grain of wheat, which he gave to the king. Now

the king was too proud to ask what this meant, so he brought the wheat back to his palace. Knowing that it must be valuable, he put it into a gold box and locked it in his safe. Every day he would open the box and look at the grain of wheat. But nothing ever happened to it, and the king became more and more puzzled.

Eventually another wise man came from out of town and visited the king. The king asked him, "What does this grain of wheat have with peace and nonviolence?" The wise man replied, "As long as you keep this grain of wheat in a box, locked in your safe, nothing is going to happen to it. It will eventually rot, and there will be nothing left. But if you were to put in the soil and allow it to interact with nature and the elements, it would grow and multiply. Soon you would have a whole field of wheat.

"In the same way, you can't keep peace and non-violence locked up in your heart and mind. You have to allow them to interact with nature and the elements. Then they will grow and multiply."

I learned the lesson my grandfather wanted to teach with that story. I also learned more. My garden taught me about being a good friend and a good relative. It taught me how you have to nurture relationships. It also taught me that in order to enjoy the fruits in life, you must work. The work is hard. Sometimes it is difficult to see progress. But seeds do grow and bear fruit.

I think that working in the garden, and associating that experience so closely with my education and philosophy, has helped me to understand and appreciate everything I encounter in life.

Admiral James O. Ellis

Commander, U.S. Naval Forces Europe

At one point in my career, I was fortunate to command the nuclear aircraft carrier U.S.S. Abraham Lincoln. Powered by two giant nuclear reactors and weighing over 100,000 tons, this was the largest, most dominant warship in the world.

This ship had the power to transition from one point to another at a high rate of speed. But sometimes, when the clouds would gather and the seas began to build quickly, I found that as I would accelerate, she would not ride well at all. She would buck. The waves would slap the hull. It was a very uncomfortable ride. As large and powerful as the ship was, I had to slow down to avoid both the discomfort and the very real possibility that if I continued to go at the maximum speed at which the ship was capable, I might actually damage her.

After being in command for a while, I began to

you proceed directly and at flying speed, you may encounter opposition. You may run into a lack of buy-in or full support. However, if you can modify your approach a little bit—not compromise your principles, but take into account the concerns of the organization and slightly alter your course to accommodate those concerns—the organization runs much more smoothly and progresses much more quickly, and ultimately you arrive at your destination with your ship and crew intact. If you don't, you may still get the job done, but the resistance will be higher. There will be unintended consequences. You may even damage other initiatives or goals of the organization.

I am convinced that it's always wise to think about a course that best serves everybody's interests. My experience has been that, in most cases, there is such a course, and ultimately it allows you to arrive at the destination with your organization intact, with morale high, and without any unintended second or third-order damages and consequences that might act to the detriment of the organization.

The best way to get to your goal is not always a straight-line approach. Sometimes success depends on your ability to alter your approach slightly to accommodate some of the realities with which you must deal—whether they are natural realities at sea or the organizational realities with which you have to contend.

experiment. I realized that if I would alter my course slightly—sometimes as little as 10 degrees in one direction or another—the ship would not only ride better, but I could go at a much faster speed and actually get to my ultimate destination at the same time or even sooner.

I found the leadership translation of this experience is that even though you may be in charge of your organization and have the authority and the power to make a decision and define the direction for that organization, if

To effectively work with change, we need to understand it, to respect it. A farmer may not understand every biochemical reaction that causes something to grow, but the more he understands the natural processes of planting, nurturing, and growth, the more productive he becomes.

Changelessness

Although *we* don't control change, *principles do.* Nature teaches that there is order in complexity. There are patterns in change. There are natural laws that are in control.

Tides change...but there are principles or dynamics upon which they change. Seeds change...but principles of growth govern their development into mature plants that bear flowers and food.

JoAnn Valenti

Author, professor, journalist

Nature just "is." It cannot be controlled. People can mess around with it. They can interfere with it. They can pollute it. They can damage it. They can degrade it. But they can never really control it. The sun will rise every day. The sun will set every day. Those mountains will be there whether you look at them or not. Nature is there, even when you don't ask it to be. It doesn't demand anything from you. It just is, and all you have to do is experience and appreciate it.

Depending on the atmosphere, the weather, and the temperature, there's a different sunset every day...but there's always a sunset.

At the very heart of nature are principles that apply everywhere in nature—including our own lives, relationships, and organizations, because we are a part of nature. So we learn from nature:

The key to dealing with change
is to have a changeless core.

To understand, trust, and live in harmony with the natural laws that govern in all of life is what produces inner peace and even some degree of predictability, even in the midst of a complex, chaotic environment.

Consider the Law of the Farm. The same law that tells you it's ludicrous to think you can goof off all spring, play all summer, throw a bunch of seeds in the ground at the beginning of fall, and reap a bountiful harvest two weeks later also tells you there's no way you're going to neglect planning and preparation, avoid building relationships, and side-step problems, and end up with a strong, effective family or organization.

It also tells you that whatever you sow, you're going to reap. If, as a leader, you sow seeds of mistrust through dishonesty, backbiting, using people, or playing political games, you're never going to reap the benefits of a high trust culture in the long run. You may experience some apparent short-term results, but they will never endure. In the long term, The Law of the Farm will govern. You simply cannot violate with impunity the laws that govern growth. In other words, if you plant weeds, you're never going to harvest peas.

Now, there will still be unknowns. Like the farmer, you can't predict exactly what will happen to your crop every year. Sometimes the unpredictability of weather and other conditions will change the time of harvest. Something in the environment may even destroy the crop.

But still you learn that if you keep preparing the soil, planting, nurturing, and doing all you can to be a wise steward, over time you will reap what you sow. Though the individual events can't always be predicted, the pattern can be predicted. If you think in terms of principles, are true to principles, and exercise faith in the results, they will eventually come to pass.

Nature is evenly balanced. We cannot disturb her equilibrium, for we know that the law of Cause and Effect is the unerring and inexorable law of nature; but we do fail to find our own equilibrium as nations and as individuals, because we have not yet learned that the same law works as inexorably in human life and in society as in nature—that what we sow, we must inevitably reap.

Sidney Bremer

Spirit of Apollo

Consider other changeless natural laws and how they affect our roles as leaders.

Interdependence

In nature, everything is related to everything else. Consider the complex interrelationship of the food chain, the microorganisms in the soil that allow plants to live, the effect of photosynthesis—of light transforming plant chlorophyll into sugar, creating food for other living things.

Anything beyond a casual glance at nature begins to reveal complex levels of interrelationship.

The problem for us as leaders comes when we look at our organization in terms of mechanical, isolated parts instead of as an organic, highly interrelated whole. Nature teaches us that businesses, families, and communities are also complex ecosystems, and that what happens in one part affects all parts. It also helps us to realize that every individual is important, and that each contributes to the welfare of all.

Growth

Nature teaches that all living things require constant nourishment and nurturing of the conditions that encourage growth. The problem comes when we forget that our own growth requires exercise and nourishment for body, mind, and spirit; when we fail to nurture the relationships and conditions that create growth; when we treat others and organizations as non-living things.

Order

Nature teaches that some things
necessarily come before other things.
The planting of the seed and nurturing
of the young plant come before the harvest
of the mature plant. Aspen groves prepare
the earth for the pine trees that follow.
In our lives and in our organizations,
algebra comes before calculus. Trust-
worthiness precedes trust. We can't
expect to have effective communication
until we create the systems and relationships that will produce it.

Balance

Nature teaches that balance is a dynamic equilibrium—a synergistic ecosystem in which all parts contribute to the effectiveness of the whole. The problem comes when we see balance in a mechanical rather than a natural way. We try to create balance in our lives by running fast enough to touch all the bases, or balance in the organization by equalizing resources spent like distributing weight on the sides of a mechanical scale. Balance does not require sameness or equality. It requires wholeness and harmony. It is diversity and interdependence that make a true dynamic equilibrium possible.

Seasons

In nature, there are seasons.
There are times of preparing and
planting, times of watering and
nurturing, times—often very intense
times—of harvest. Although some
are seasons of imbalance, each
season contributes to the balance
of the whole. Our lives and our
organizations also have seasons.
A new baby, a new business, a new
challenge may create seasons of
imbalance. But effectively handled,
even these seasons of imbalance
help to create the balance of
the whole.

Opposition

Nature teaches the value of opposition and challenge. The turbulent stream purifies the water. By pushing against its cocoon, the butterfly gains sufficient strength to fly. In our own lives and organizations, exercising our muscles—physical, mental, or moral—gives us strength and prevents atrophy. The leader learns to learn from the challenges, failures, and problems of life to improve life.

As the tree is fertilized by its own broken branches and fallen leaves and grows out of its own decay, so men and nations are bettered and improved by trial and refined out of broken hopes and blighted expectations.

F. W. Robinson

I thought of the lessons [the sea] had taught us as children. A certain amount of patience (you can't hurry the tides). A great deal of respect (the sea does not suffer fools gladly). An awareness of the vast and mysterious interdependence of things (wind and tide and current, calm and squall and hurricane, all combining to determine the paths of the birds above and the fish below). And the cleanness of it all, with every beach swept twice a day by the great broom of the sea.

Arthur Gordon

A Touch of Wonder

Hyrum Smith

Author, Chairman, Franklin Covey Co.

I grew up in Hawaii, and I spent a lot of time in the waves. I learned to gain a great respect for the power of the ocean. Sometimes it's easy to think, "I'm all powerful." But then you get thrashed by a 15-foot wave, and you realize, "Maybe I'm not as powerful as I thought."

Several near-death experiences with large waves had a real impact on me as I was growing up. I began to recognize that there are powers out there that are much greater than you. There are forces out there—natural laws, if you will. And if you don't make the conscious decision to live by those laws, there are going to be painful consequences.

Now, this is by no means a comprehensive list of the principles nature teaches, nor is it intended to be. We only give these few as examples.

The point is that these natural laws or principles do exist, and that there are an infinite number of applications of each of these principles in our leadership roles. To understand this is to open the door to a

whole new way of seeing, learning, and living. And to live with integrity to these principles provides a powerful source of inner peace and strength.

If there are overarching principles that give organization to the myriad of multi-level principles we see in the natural world, they would be the three constants— change, changelessness, and choice.

Within that framework, the leadership lessons of nature are all around us. They teach us the laws that govern in leadership and in life. And they teach us in a way that is unique and personal, in the way we need to know.

Choice

The third constant—choice—is the summum bonum of human capacity. It is the fundamental leadership activity. It empowers us to deal effectively with change and changelessness.

Though human beings are not the only entities in nature that have choice, it's clear that at least two things about human choice are unique.

The first is that humans have the widest scope of choice. At the same time, they are capable of the most degrading and the most beautiful and uplifting acts in all of nature.

The second is that humans have moral choice. It is the scope and nature of human choice that give us the responsibility of respectful stewardship with regard to the rest of creation.

Our ability to choose affirms that each of us is a leader. Every day we make choices that affect the direction of our lives, our families, our organizations, our communities. When choices are made with little or no understanding of natural law, they tend to be simplistic, reactionary, myopic, or egotistical. The cost is extreme. At the core, almost every personal or organizational failure can be traced to poor decision-making.

But when we learn to make choices

Stedman Graham

Author, President and CEO, SGA

I was visiting at my aunt's house the other day, sitting out on the porch, and I said, "You know, I'm doing all of this stuff, but you are the one who is really enjoying life. You are the one who has it all." She's not out there every day trying to create successful opportunities and build an empire, but she can sit on her porch and enjoy the hummingbirds, the pure air, the tranquillity. She is close to the earth and close to the environment, and it doesn't get any better than that.

I don't care how successful or wealthy you become or how many achievements you develop, the greatest feeling you can get is to be able to go back to the purest form of nature, to walk on the grass, to be around the trees. Nature gets you away from the stress, from all the busy-ness you create in your life when you go everywhere to go nowhere. You're able to think and be more intro-spective. You get to look within yourself and create a peaceful environment.

And without that quality time, you don't think. You don't get a chance to really plan. You just react, and then you're in crisis management all the time and you make mistakes. You make quick decisions without planning or preparation. You don't really think about the vision you want and how it's going to play out.

based on timeless principles—to handle change and create change based on changeless natural laws—we create posi-tive results. Our choices reflect wisdom and lead to contribution. We recognize that others, too, have choice. We tend to lead in ways that respect that choice— ways that release human potential rather than trying to control behavior.

For leaders, choice is where the rubber meets the road.

So how can we learn to make better choices?

We can choose to value principles. We can choose to look beneath the thin veneer of social conditioning and deep into the true nature of life and leadership. We can look for principles, seek to really understand and apply them, and live in harmony with them.

Principles control consequences;
Values control behavior.

The more our values are in harmony with principles, the better decisions we will make...and the more inner peace we will have.

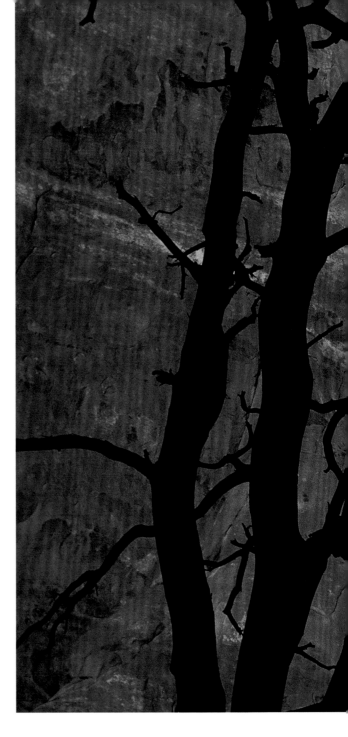

Alan O'Neill

Superintendent, Lake Mead National Recreation Area

About three years ago, I was feeling really disconnected. I got into meditation and other things to help me get rid of the rapid head talk and connect with who I was from the inside. But quite frankly, despite my intentions and best efforts, I was having difficulty making that connection.

So I prepared myself to take a three-day vision quest on a mountain. I asked a friend of mine who was familiar with such quests to help me prepare. I planned to fast. I carried water, a sleeping bag, and a journal—and that was it. I asked for guidance. I asked for whatever experiences I

needed to receive. I asked to be able to walk through my own fears.

Only 10 minutes into the journey, I had my first lesson. I heard a rattle and saw a snake strike at my walking stick about six inches from my foot. For a moment, fear overwhelmed me. But then I remembered that everything on this journey was supposed to be a lesson for my understanding and growth, so I tried to step back from my fear and learn. The snake curled up on a large boulder that was close to me. As I stood still and looked at it, I had a sudden, powerful paradigm shift. It was almost as if I established instant communication with that snake, and I felt overwhelmed

with what I was experiencing.

No longer was the snake something to be feared. I saw its oneness with nature. I saw the beauty in it, and I started thinking, "If I can accept the beauty in this snake, what is it within my own being that I am fearing and not accepting?"

I also recognized that all things are equal in creation, and that the fear of the unknown leads to pre-judgment of things that are different. I began to better understand the issue of wholeness, the connection of everything to the divine.

In the late afternoon, I watched an incredible sunset. The intensity of this sunset was beyond anything I had ever seen. I asked, "What am I to learn from this?" And the answer came in waves of emotion, almost like the waves of the ocean. It was all about opening my heart, opening myself up to experiences and to other people.

After a while, I noticed that a storm was moving in. As it started to become intense, I began to be fearful. There was thunder and lightning everywhere around me. The mountain was deluged with rain. It was the most intense storm I had ever experienced, and I have seen quite a few.

But I felt inside that at some level, I was protected. I had wanted to walk through my own fears, and the universe was giving me exactly what I had asked for.

The storm lasted for about two hours where I was, but I stayed up all night watching it play out around me. It was incredibly beautiful.

The lesson for me was that fear is a state of thought,

but at a deeper level, we have to know that we are always protected. Whether we are in the midst of a storm at work or whatever we are involved in in our lives, at some level we have to allow ourselves to be calm because we know it's all going to be okay. It was an incredible lesson in trust.

The next day, as I looked in the crevices of the rocks on top of the mountain, I found tens of thousands of lady-bugs—all piled on top of each other in a state of sleep. I thought they were dead, but I poked them and they moved. As I was trying to figure out the lesson, I realized that nature was saying, "Look at how these ladybugs are supporting each other in this perfect state." The only way to fill the gap was for each to support the others.

Later on, I looked up and saw an eagle overhead. It was circling me, spiraling down and then up, and then down and then up, again and again. The message to me was to free myself. On many levels, I had turned control of my life over to other people and had not realized it. I was over-committed to everyone. I couldn't say "no." I was serving on boards and service clubs, and had allowed myself to lose balance. I needed to take back personal responsibility and gather my courage to do what was necessary so that I could soar above the mundane levels of my life. I also needed to face my fears and move past them, to look beyond the horizon of what was presently available, and to free myself from what bound me.

I watched ants on an ant hill for half an hour or so. The message was that these ants had a plan. I didn't know what that plan was, but I could see there was a commitment of the community or team to that plan, and that they were following it. Since they could only do small pieces of it at a time, there was also a message of patience—that dreams are fulfilled incrementally, one step at a time.

On the final morning I woke up, and there—in the midst of the desert at 6,500 feet—I was absolutely bathed in mist. I felt so peaceful, so loved and cared for and supported.

The underlying message to me was that we are always loved and provided for, no matter where we are.

This experience has had a profound impact on me as an individual. Even though I had some sense of what I needed to do, I was having a hard time doing it in an urban setting. It was stepping out in nature and allowing the rhythm and the elements of nature to speak that empowered me to clearly define it and to do it. I had a clarity there that I had never had in my life.

It's also had a dramatic impact on me as a leader. The experience with the snake has taught me not to fear. Where before I had a lot of well-masked fear—about everything from speaking in front of a group to dealing with upset stakeholders or people who relied on power and control—I can honestly say now that there's really nothing that I am fearful of in the work environment. My response is totally different.

The sunset taught me to open up to others, particularly to the staff. And because I'm open, they're willing to open up, too, and it really makes a difference in how we operate. I've found that sometimes you just have to be vulnerable and not worry about whether people will think you're crazy or not.

The storm taught me to be calm in the midst of other storms. Now, when people are very reactive on the job and it looks like things are really starting to unravel, I find I can step back and calmly give a different perspective. I can say, "Hey, folks, this too shall pass. Let's not put our energy into this; let's put it into something else." And we move right past it.

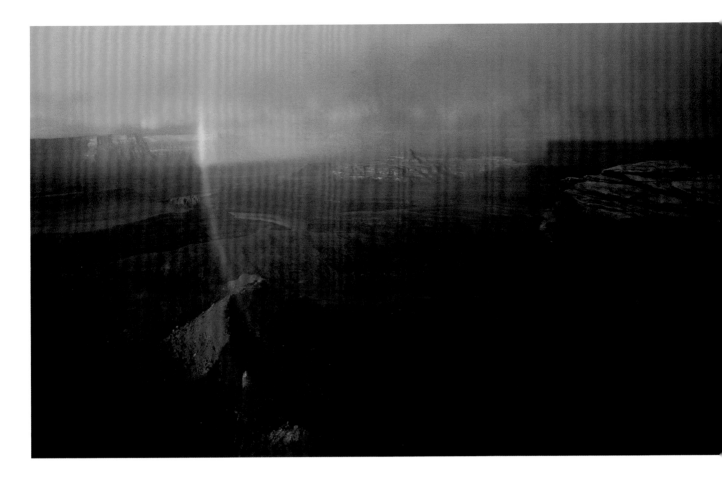

The ladybugs helped me learn that everyone is special, that everyone's role is important. In our organization now, we constantly remind ourselves of that fact. Although we still award people individually, most of the things we make the big splash over are collective accomplishments and celebrations of the role every person plays. At the end of the fiscal year, for example, we have a huge celebration of what we accomplished together during the year. We produce a video of about 700 pictures taken throughout the year and put it to music, and the response is overwhelming. People are actually fighting back tears. And the whole idea comes back to the ladybugs. Everyone's role really is key, and we put the emphasis on what we can accomplish when the whole team works together.

I am convinced that our lessons come from everywhere, and that whether it's a rock, a tree, a bird, or whatever, everything within the environment has something to teach us if we will only take the time to listen.

We can work to gain more accurate perspective.

Dewitt Jones

The first decision I have to make as a photographer is, "What lens do I have on my camera?" In other words, what perspective will I view the problem from to find a creative solution? I know that if I don't have the right perspective going in, I don't have a chance of finding the extraordinary view.

I use this metaphor regularly in the rest of my life as well. I'm always asking myself in my business or in my relationship with my community or my family, "Do I have the right perspective? Do I have the right point of view?"

Sometimes I find I need my telephoto lens to go in and pick just those few elements out of the cacophony of life which will afford me an extraordinary perspective. At other times, I need a wide-angle lens. I need to see the big picture, the strategic view that gives greater context to the problem. How often in business do we to need to step back and see the forest as well as the trees?

Jake Garn

Former U.S. Senator,

Space Shuttle Discovery Flight Crew Member

The effect of going out into space was incredible! No matter how many pictures we had seen before, no matter now much training we'd had, we were not prepared for that first view of the earth. The first time I had the opportunity to look out, I thought my heart and lungs had stopped. It was just beyond any imagination I'd had of what it would look like.

The seven of us on board represented five different religions. But we were all agreed—it just doesn't make sense how people on earth treat each other. It doesn't make any difference what language we speak. It doesn't make any difference what country we come from. It certainly doesn't make any difference what the color of our skin is. We are all children of God traveling on spaceship earth together.

There is no doubt that the perspective of seeing an entire natural environment all at one time has changed my life. To put it bluntly, I am a nicer person. I am more considerate. I am more willing to work with people. I am softer in my leadership and how I try to achieve things. It has had a very profound effect on my life, my appreciation of this earth, the value of people, and how we should treat each other as God's children, regardless of our differences ethnically, religiously, or in any other way.

Richard A. Searfoss

Lieutenant Colonel, U.S. Air Force; NASA Astronaut

The incomparable sights of the thin line of the atmosphere with its multiple hues of blue darkening to the deepest black of space, startling, brilliant orbital sunrises, and night thunderstorms over the tropics popping off like dozens of flashbulbs all speak of sublime beauty, wonder, hope, and infinite power. Of the literally thousands of looks at planet Earth I've had, never once was I not deeply touched and correspondingly humbled, trying as it were to take a sip from a veritable firehose from which coursed a deluge of splendid, ever changing views witnessing to the grand glory of God's planetary creation. This planet is indeed full of infinite wonders. We should be grateful to call it home.

Stedman Graham

Author, President and CEO, SGA

What nature represents to me is diversity. There are so many different kinds of animals, plants, mountains, and bodies of water that make up the whole world. The beauty is in the sum of the parts that equals the whole.

And I believe it's the same thing in life. It's the diversity that makes a company or a community or this country really great—the sum of the parts. And when you're in a position where the parts are not up to par and there's an imbalance in the parts, then the whole is affected.

So we need to protect the parts. The key to a strong family, for example, is to work on developing strong members of the family so that the sum of the family members equals a strong family structure. And the same thing is true in communities and organizations.

We can choose to value interdependence, to believe that there is more than one "right" answer, and to value the diversity that creates synergy.

I point my lens into a field of flowers. A thousand fantastic shapes and colors all designed for one purpose: to propagate the seed of the mother plant. I shoot roll upon roll of film, covering this small patch of ground from every angle, with every lens. I come away with a hundred great photographs.

What have I learned? Both from nature and from the practice of my craft, the answer springs loud and clear: "There's more than one right answer!"

did so not in fear, but comfortably, knowing that it would be there for me. Slowly, I began to embrace change rather than fear it.

Most important, I began to approach the world with a sense of abundance rather than scarcity. The lesson of "more than one right answer" pointed me in this direction, but it was nature's lesson of beauty that confirmed it. Nature plants beauty everywhere—in the clouds, in the light on the mountains, in the pattern of dead leaves on

We are raised to believe that there are single right answers. Hundreds of multiple choice tests in school; give the right answer, you get an A; give the wrong answer, you flunk. But nature doesn't see it that way. It finds thousands of solutions to the challenges it faces, thousands of "right answers."

When I began to embrace what nature seemed to be teaching, both my perspective and my actions began to change. I no longer stopped at the first right answer. And when I pressed out, looking for that next right answer, I

the forest floor, in her tiniest seed. It is always there, if I am open enough to see it.

Once you discover that there is more than one "right answer" in life and in leadership, you begin to celebrate the things that lead to multiple right answers, such as the diversity of your work force or the concept of empowerment. You realize that good ideas can come from anywhere, and that everyone has something to contribute based on his or her own point of view.

We can choose to nurture our relationship with nature, including our relationships with other people. We can be good stewards of the earth. We can realize that the way we treat nature—particularly animals—is often one of the best mirrors of our relationships with others, as well as a mirror of our own souls. If our paradigm in nature is one of command and control, our paradigm in life and leadership is likely the same. But which paradigm makes for better leadership—seeking to control others or seeking to release the potential and creativity within?

Susan Butcher

Three-time (and first female) winner of the Iditarod sled race

One spring day early in my career, I was taking my team on a trail that crossed a frozen river—the same trail we had used almost daily all winter long. As we started across the river, my lead dog suddenly veered to the right. I gave her the command to go left and she went back for me, but then she immediately veered off to the right again. Several times I tried to get her back on the trail, and each time she responded the same way. I couldn't figure out what was happening. She had never disobeyed me before. Finally I went ahead and let her have the lead, and just as she pulled me and the team off to the side of the trail, the entire river collapsed! Her sixth sense saved our lives.

Since that time, I've learned that a lot of leadership is about teamwork. I usually have about 10 leaders in a 15-dog team, and one of the leaders will let me know, "Hey, we're getting into a storm. This is not my bag. Can you get me out of the lead?" And another member of the team will tell me, "I love this stuff! Put me up there." They are constantly changing off the lead based on who is most adept to handle a particular problem.

I own and run a business, and this has certainly helped me to know that when I am dealing with something that I may not be the best expert in, I can turn to my employees and let them take the lead. Success is a total team effort, and it sometimes takes letting go and trusting in the talents and instincts of those whose "paws are on the ice," so to speak.

Hazel O'Leary

Chairman, Keystone Energy Group;

Former U.S. Secretary of Energy

More than a decade ago, my husband Jack died suddenly. He had been vigorous physically, mentally, and spiritually. Neither I nor the rest of the family were prepared for his death, and we had difficulty reconciling our loss.

Just prior to his death, Jack and I had built a new home. The landscape design had been our joint project, and now the plan had to be implemented without him. Clearing, planting, and cultivating had to be done in every corner of the property. So I dug into the earth and ripped out debris with a passion. I planted and watered. And little by little, I found myself healing. By the time the plants and flowers started to grow, I was watching them with almost a fascination. I realized that they were teaching me about life and death, about growth and rebirth. I came to understand that life is a cycle, and that death is an important part of that cycle.

I spent hours in the garden every day. And I knew that while I was helping the plants and flowers to grow, they were helping me to heal. The garden, though fragile and

in need of support, was strong enough to withstand the seasonal changes and the storms. The beauty of a garden is in its response to our care and attention. A garden well cared for will endure.

The lessons taught in the garden of living, supporting, learning—and yes, even dying—give us certainty that we are not necessarily in charge.

Now, with faith and the support of family and friends, I have begun a new garden in a new place. And shortly, this garden will be shared with a new companion, a man whose love of nature and its gifts complements my own. Even late in life, I have discovered, there can be a new beginning.

And, although we cannot choose what happens to us, we can choose our response to what happens to us.

In making these kinds of choices, we become principle-centered leaders—people who live and lead others based on the natural laws of effectiveness that govern in all of life. And making those positive choices is the difference between being a leader and a victim.

Everything stress is, gardening is not. Stress is hurried and harried; gardening has the pace of nature's season-long rhythms. Stress is feeling powerless and victimized; gardening is control over both your food supply and your immediate environment. Stress is alienation, isolation; gardening is taking part in the great cycles of the earth, the cycles of growth and nourishment, or death and rebirth; it is a daily and joyous ritual of participation in the unity of life. As you garden, you are healed—body and mind, heart and soul.

Organic Gardening

Mit Romney

Founder and CEO, Bain Capital, Inc.

The responsibility of running a company is intrinsically very self-centering and self-aggrandizing. As a CEO, you adjust people's compensation, you're responsible for promotions and dismissals, you watch the earnings of the company and take responsibility for fluctuations based on the wisdom of your decisions. As a result, it's easy to become convinced that you stand at the center of the universe.

But nature has the power to put things in a more proper perspective. Two summers ago, my family and I went down the Colorado River. As we prepared to sleep out in the valley of the Grand Canyon, we were made very aware of our place in the universe. When you think about the eons of time represented by the canyons around you, the ever-flowing river at your feet, and the heavens above, something says to you that what you are about in your job just isn't that important. The relationships we have with God and with our fellow beings take on far more significance.

In the scheme of eternity, our time on earth is just a moment. We are here for just the blink of an eye, and then we are gone. I think that perspective allows one to experience life, business, and work in a much more calm and less frantic way.

The Result

As we open to nature, people, and principles, we find the Sundance Promise fulfilled: We get what we need—personally, individually, specifically—to be better leaders.

We also become more humble, more teachable, more aware of our place in creation.

Dick Roth

Olympic Swimmer, Gold Medalist,

Former World Record Holder

One of the highlights of my life was winning the

Olympic gold medal and setting a world record in the

400-meter individual medley in swimming. Through the

events that led up to this experience, I learned to focus,

sacrifice, accept responsibility, and apply principles to

accomplish significant results.

But after the Olympics, I realized that it was possible

to climb to the top and still have a whole lot of living left to do. I wondered if material victories were really going to be satisfying. I struggled to decide whether I should go out and earn money or try to win the race in some other way. I finally decided to simplify my life, to focus more on the inward journey and pursue something more integrated, more in line with that focus.

I eventually ended up working on a 585,000 acre ranch, and that experience really put a lot of things in perspective. I discovered there was no way to rise above nature, to conquer it. It was so vast, so immense, so unarguably "there" with the changing of seasons, the incredible storms, the grasses that grow every year. I felt a greater sense of context, of the "big picture" and my place in it.

I spent several years on that ranch, and it was a wonderful time in my life. But then, after all that time living and learning in nature, I thought, "Okay, now how does this apply?" It's easy to see principles when you're in nature. With the stars, the sky, the river, you can't miss it. But it's more of a challenge to integrate it in the world of human beings, where you get confounded by people problems and you don't see natural principles so easily. I felt I needed to get back into the stream of life, to understand and integrate some of my learnings in the human realm. I realized that after the ranch, there was still a lot of living left to do.

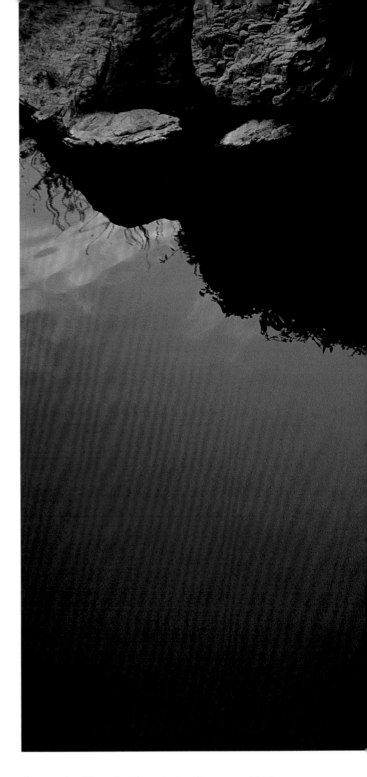

We feel harmony and peace. We feel the power of principles. Insights and answers come. And we are filled with gratitude for nature, for people, and for the principles that give meaning to leadership and to life.

Dewitt Jones

As I look through my lenses, nature presents me with an abundance of beauty beyond my wildest imaginings. Over and over again, she seems to be saying, "Relax. There is more here than you will ever need. When you believe it, you will see it."

The more I believe it, the more I do see it...not just in "nature," but in my family, in my profession, and in myself. It fills me with gratitude—and happiness. That shouldn't surprise me. Philosopher and lecturer Dennis Prager writes:

The factor that most determines our happiness is...
gratitude. It's very simple: the more you're grateful
for, the happier you will be; the less you're grateful
for, the less happy you will be.

Gratitude...how many times have I clicked off a shot of a dew drop, or a sunset, or a child, and, as I lower my camera, found myself silently murmuring, "Thank you!" Those flashes of gratitude help illuminate the rest of my life. Glancing at a field as I drive down the freeway, I feel a smile pull at my lips as my mind's eye delights in the

thousands of breathtaking photos I know are hidden there. So I can't stop to take them—the fact that I know they're there makes that field a little more special.

Each time nature helps me get in touch with the extraordinariness of this world, my gratitude—my happiness—increases.

You don't have to go to the far ends of the earth to find it. Recently I was in the lobby of the Ventana Resort in Tucson, Arizona. I was there speaking to a corporate audience about how to increase creativity in the work-

place. During a break I stepped out on the balcony with a simple point-and-shoot camera I had with me and gazed down into a small pool below. What I saw seemed a southwestern version of the biblical burning bush. A single saguaro glowing with the late afternoon sun was reflected in the liquid darkness. Like the biblical bush, the cactus didn't demand that I look at it; it merely invited me to. I raised the camera and took the invitation. Through the viewfinder I delighted in the contrast between the fiery cactus and the cool blue rocks on the shore. Then that

sense of gratitude filled me again, that inner "Thank you!" at being allowed to witness such a sight.

Perhaps the greatest lesson we can learn from nature is gratitude. If we could publish it in our lives everyday, the way nature publishes beauty in every sunrise and every sunset, how different might the world be?

As we conclude this book, we encourage you to claim the Sundance Promise for yourself. Make the proactive choice to create a deep and meaningful relationship with nature, people, and principles. When you feel challenged or you begin to feel overwhelmed, discouraged, anxious, road-blocked, or out of balance in any arena of life, reconnect with the ever-present reminders of change, changelessness, and choice that are all around you. Be truly open. Seek wisdom. Ask the hard questions. Ponder deeply.

The answers will come. And in carrying them out, you will become a more effective leader in all arenas of your life.

That's "the nature of leadership!"

'Night is drawing nigh'—

For all that has been—Thanks!

To all that shall be—Yes!

Dag Hammarskjold

119

Photo Notes

Dewitt Jones

Photography is a discipline that shapes both my vision and my values. It brings me into the deepest contact with the natural world and allows me to experience the lessons nature has to teach. Through the lens I learn to transform the ordinary into the extraordinary, and that is the key—to creativity, to leadership, to life.

Cover
*Leaves,
Selkirk Mountains,
British Columbia,
Canada*

Page 2-3
*Sun Flowers,
Northern Utah*

Page 4-5
*Slocan Lake, Valhalla
Mountains, British
Columbia, Canada*

Page 9
*Havasu Creek, Grand
Canyon National
Park, Arizona*

Page 10
*Redwood forest,
Eureka, California*

Page 18
*Leaves,
Selkirk Mountains,
British Columbia,
Canada*

Page 19
*Dawn, Point Reyes
National Seashore,
California*

Page 22-23
*Pines and reflections,
Glacier National Park,
Montana*

Page 24-25
*Tree reflected in lake,
Yellowstone National
Park, Wyoming*

Page 28
*Kanab Creek, Grand
Canyon National
Park, Arizona*

Page 30-31
*Breaking storm,
Nice, France*

Page 31
*Flowers after rain,
Cortez Island, British
Columbia, Canada*

Page 33
*Redwood in the lifting
mist, Redwoods
National Park,
California*

Page 34-35
*Clam diggers,
Bodega Bay,
California*

Page 35
*Farm and setting
moon near Great
Falls, Montana*

Page 36-37
*Tuloumne Meadows,
Yosemite National
Park, California*

Page 38
*Coastal mountain
near Half Moon Bay,
California*

Page 38-39
*Dolphin in the
Johnston Strait,
British Columbia,
Canada*

Page 40-41
*Wheat fields near
Livermore, California*

Page 41
*Wave foam, Point
Reyes National
Seashore, California*

Page 42
*Apples at harvest time,
New Denver, British
Columbia, Canada*

Page 43
*Saint Mary Lake,
Glacier National Park,
Montana*

Page 44-45
*Young Woodpecker,
Sequoia National
Park, California*

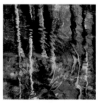
Page 46
*Reflections, Yosemite
Creek, Yosemite
National Park,
California*

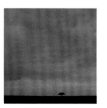
Page 46-47
*Acacia Tree, Serengeti
National Park,
Tanzania, Africa*

Page 48
Ferns, Molokai, Hawaii

Page 50
Gambel's Oak Leaf, Coral Pink Sand Dunes State Park, Utah

Page 51
Dead log with fungus, Coastal Mountains, California

Page 52-53
Valhalla Provincial Park, British Columbia, Canada

Page 54
Crystal Rapids, Colorado River, Grand Canyon National Park, Arizona

Page 55
Snow Geese, Sacramento National Wildlife Refuge, California

Page 57
Dories on the Colorado River, Grand Canyon National Park, Arizona

Page 60
Vineyard, Napa Valley, California

Page 60-61
Wine grapes, Napa Valley, California

Page 63
Wheat field, Nice, France

Page 64-65
The Great Beach, Point Reyes National Seashore, California

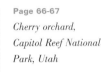

Page 66-67
Cherry orchard, Capitol Reef National Park, Utah

Page 68-69
Stinson Beach, Marin County, California

Page 69
Seed, Thetford Center, Vermont

Page 70-71
Sunset, South Moresby National Park Reserve, British Columbia, Canada

Page 73
(top) Winter sunset, Yellowstone National Park, Wyoming

Page 75
New Denver, British Columbia, Canada

Page 76-77
Burnaby Narrows, South Moresby National Park Reserve, British Columbia, Canada

Page 78
Pine boughs, Coastal Mountains, California

Page 79
Bird of Paradise stem, Molokai, Hawaii

Page 80
Birch Trees, Boulder Mountain, Utah

Page 81
Spider web and sun, Bolinas, California

Page 84-85
(both) Lower Yosemite Falls, Yosemite National Park, California

Page 87
Eagle Falls, Lake Tahoe, California

Page 88-89
Dawn waves, Moro Bay, California

Page 90
Star trails (long exposure), Zion National Park, Utah

Page 92-93
Porch, Molokai, Hawaii

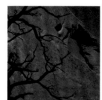

Page 94-95

*Skyline Arch,
Arches National Park,
Moab, Utah*

Page 95

*Rattlesnake,
Rockville, Utah*

Page 96-97

*The West Temple,
Zion National Park,
Utah*

Page 97

*Dead Horse Point
State Park,
Moab, Utah*

Page 98-99

*Eagle, Graham Island,
Queen Charlotte
Islands,
British Columbia,
Canada*

Page 100

*The Race Track,
Death Valley
National Monument,
California*

Page 101

*Winter,
Yellowstone
National Park,
Wyoming*

Page 105

*(top) Maple leaves
in creek bed,
Zion National Park,
Utah*

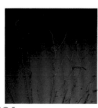

Page 105

*(bottom) Ocotillo
blooms, Anza-Borrego
Desert State Park,
California*

Page 106

*Clover and lupine field,
Tehachapi Range,
Central Valley,
California*

Page 107

*Lupine,
Sierra foothills,
California*

Page 110-111

*Garden, Hollyhock
Farm, Cortez Island,
British Columbia,
Canada*

Page 111

*Flower,
Edinburgh,
Scotland*

Page 112

*Convict Lake, Sierra
Nevada, California*

Page 113

*Colorado River,
Grand Canyon
National Park,
Arizona*

Page 114-115

*Autumn, Bob
Marshall Wilderness,
Montana*

Page 116-117

*Saguaro Cactus
reflection, Ventana
Resort, Tucson,
Arizona*

Roger Merrill

For me, photography has been a great gift. It's all about light and how to see light. Through creation's light, all of life is illuminated.

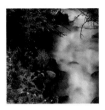

Page 1
Antelope Canyon, Arizona

Page 7
Mount Timpanogos, Utah

Page 12-13
Provo River near Sundance, Utah

Page 14-15
Mount Timpanogos, Utah

Page 16-17
Capitol Reef National Park, Utah

Page 20-21
Stewart Falls, Sundance, Utah

Page 27
Upper New York State

Page 58-59
Tidepool, Carmel, California

Page 72
Bear Lake, Utah

Page 73
(bottom) Jasper Lake Area, Alberta, Canada

Page 82-83
Balance Rock, Arches National Park, Utah

Page 86-87
Aspen Grove, Utah

Page 99
Dead Horse Point, Utah

Page 104
Women's Memorial Garden, Nauvoo, Illinois

Page 118-119
Sunset at Fish Lake, Utah

Page 119
San Diego, California

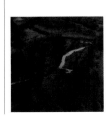

Page 120-121
Lake Powell, Utah

Page 127
Mount Timpanogos, Utah

Back Cover
High Uintahs, Utah

Jeff Schultz • Alaska Stock

Page 108
Alaska Range, interior Alaska, Dog musher mushing glacier

Page 109
South-central Alaska, Dog team on trail

National Aeronautics and Space Administration (NASA)

Page 102
Taken on board MIR space station, sunrise, Central Pacific Ocean by Andrew S. W. Thomas

Page 102-103
Indian Ocean from Apollo 11 Command Module on approach from the moon

About Franklin Covey Co.

Franklin Covey is a 4,500 member international leadership firm whose mission is to inspire change by igniting the power of proven principles so that people and organizations achieve what matters most. Franklin Covey's vision is to be the premier personal and organizational effectiveness firm in the world, impacting millions of lives each year and building a great enduring company — a model of what they teach.

Their client portfolio includes eighty-two of the Fortune 100 companies, more than two-thirds of the Fortune 500 companies, thousands of small and midsize companies, and government entities at local, state, and national levels. Franklin Covey has also created pilot partnerships with cities seeking to become principle-centered communities, and is currently teaching the 7 Habits to teachers and administrators in more than 3,500 school districts and universities nationwide and through statewide initiatives with education leaders in twenty-seven states.

Franklin Covey's approach is to teach people to teach themselves and become independent of the company. This empowerment process is carried out through programs conducted at facilities in the Rocky Mountains of Utah, custom consulting services, personal coaching, custom on-site training, and client-facilitated training, as well as through open enrollment workshops and speeches in over five hundred cities in North American and forty countries worldwide.

With more than nineteen thousand licensed client facilitators teaching its curriculum within their organizations, Franklin Covey trains in excess of 750,000 participants annually. Implementation tools, including the Franklin Planner and a wide offering of audio and video tapes, books, and computer software programs, enable clients to retain and effectively utilize concepts and skills. These and other products carefully selected and endorsed by Franklin Covey are available in more than 130 Franklin Covey stores throughout North America and in several other countries.

Products and materials are now available in thirty-two languages and their planner products are used by more than fifteen million individuals worldwide. The company has over fifteen million books in print, with more than one and a half million sold each year.

For more information on the Franklin Covey store or international office nearest you, or for a free catalog of Franklin Covey products and programs, call or write:

Franklin Covey Co.
2200 West Parkway Boulevard
Salt Lake City, Utah 84119-2331 USA
Toll Free: 800-842-2384 • Fax: 801-496-4252
International calls: 801-975-1776

For information regarding the photos or speeches by Roger Merrill or Dewitt Jones, call Franklin Covey's speakers bureau at (801) 496-5408.

Internet: http://www.franklincovey.com

One touch of nature makes the whole world kin.

Shakespeare